Violin Accompaniment

MW00446926

Violin Star 2

31 progressive pieces for beginner to Grade 1 violinists

Contents

Slurs (two crotchets per bow)
Dotted crotchet/quaver rhythms
Gypsy Fiddle   Edward Huws Jones [EHJ] (b.1948)   3
Floating By   EHJ   4
Havana Breeze   EHJ   5
The Dancing Master   17th-century English   6

Fourth finger
Ride on a Quad Bike   EHJ   7
Spring Song   Hungarian   8
Beethoven Boogie   Beethoven (1770–1827)   9
Jingle Bells   Pierpont (1822–93)   10

D major scale and arpeggio: one octave
Pachelbel's Canon   Pachelbel (1653–1706)   11
Morning Has Broken   Scottish   12

Slurs (three crotchets per bow)
Caribbean Moonlight   EHJ   13
Old-Time Waltz   English   14

Second finger position (0-12-3)
Ukulele Sam   EHJ   15
Action Hero!   EHJ   16
Action Hero! Improvisation   EHJ   18
Buzz, Buzz, Buzz
   Hoffmann von Fallersleben (1798–1874)   20
Harpist's Fingers   Welsh   21
A North Country Lass   17th-century English   22

First and second finger position (0-1-23 and 0-12-3)
G major scale and arpeggio: two octaves
Sweet Dreams   EHJ   23
Meha's Song   South Indian   24
John Ryan's Polka   Irish   25
Jewish Dance   Klezmer   26

Ties and hooked bowing
Lullaby   Weber (1786–1826)   28
Galliard   Susato (c.1510–c.70)   29

E natural minor
Bourrée from Limousin   French   30

Semiquavers
Hen-Coop Rag   EHJ   32
The Duke of Lorraine's March
   17th-century English   34
Little Brown Jug   J.Winner (1837–1918)   35

Grade 1 repertoire pieces
Hand in Hand   Mozart (1756–91)   36
Greek Wedding   Greek   37
Casey Jones   North American   38
The Boat to Inverie   EHJ   39

When a *Violin Star* piece has been selected for use in an ABRSM Violin syllabus, only the piano accompaniment from this book will be accepted in the exam room.

Book and cover design by Kate Benjamin
Music origination by Andrew Jones Notation

Printed in England by Caligraving Ltd, Thetford, Norfolk

Published in 2011 by ABRSM (Publishing) Ltd, a wholly owned subsidiary of ABRSM
© 2011 by The Associated Board of the Royal Schools of Music

Reprinted in 2015

ISBN 978 1 86096 903 4
AB 3384V

All rights reserved. No part of this publication may be reproduced, stored in a retrieval system, or transmitted in any form or by any means, electronic, mechanical, photocopying, recording, or otherwise, without the prior permission of the copyright owner.

DO NOT PHOTOCOPY
© MUSIC

Gypsy Fiddle

Floating By

Havana Breeze

The Dancing Master

17th-century English

Like a courtly dance ♩ = c.108

AB 3384V

Ride on a Quad Bike

Spring Song

Hungarian

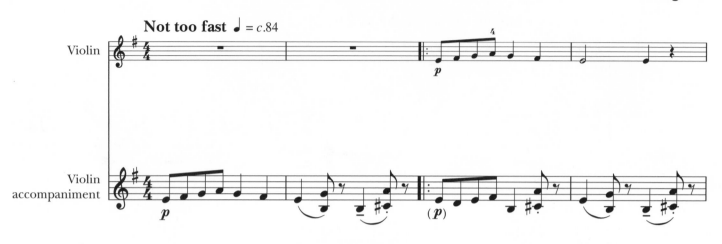

AB 3384V

Beethoven Boogie

Beethoven
(1770–1827)

Jingle Bells

Pierpont
(1822–93)

Pachelbel's Canon

Pachelbel
(1653–1706)

Morning Has Broken

Scottish

Caribbean Moonlight

Old-Time Waltz

English

Ukulele Sam

Action Hero!

Action Hero! Improvisation

Buzz, Buzz, Buzz

Hoffmann von Fallersleben
(1798–1874)

AB 3384V

Harpist's Fingers

Welsh

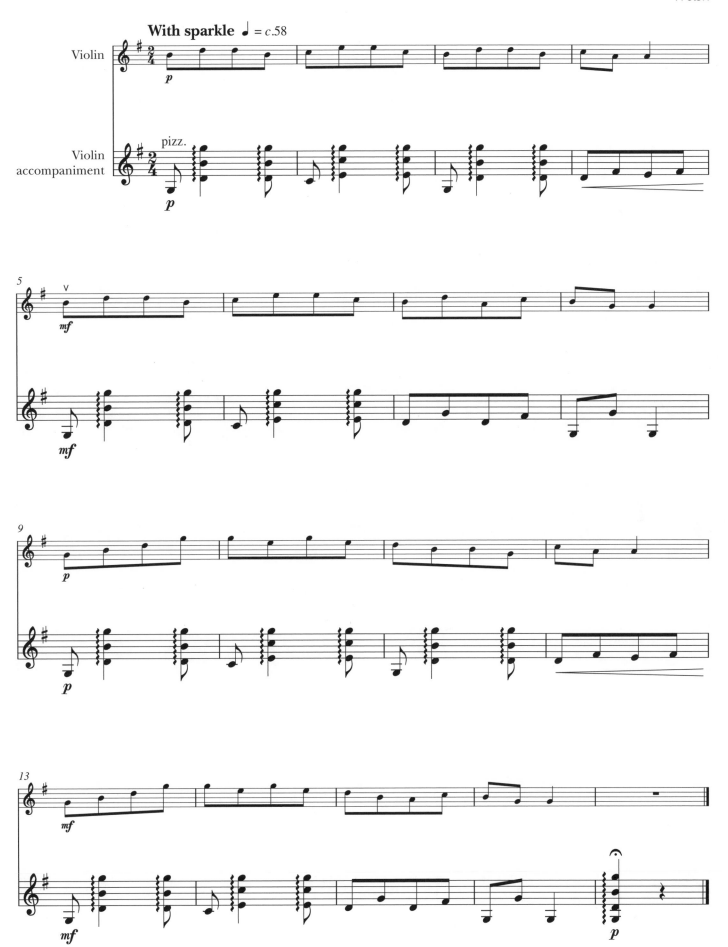

A North Country Lass

17th-century English

Sweet Dreams

Meha's Song

South Indian

John Ryan's Polka

Irish

Jewish Dance

Klezmer

Lullaby

Weber
(1786–1826)

AB 3384V

Galliard

Susato
(c.1510 – c.70)

Bourrée from Limousin

French

Hen-Coop Rag

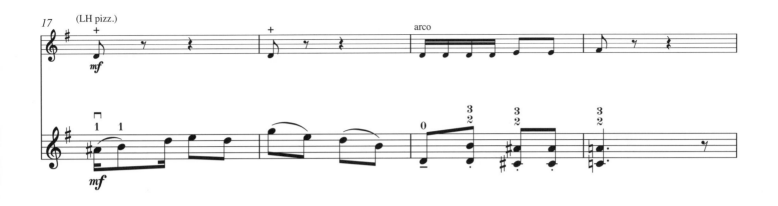

D.C. al Fine

The Duke of Lorraine's March

17th-century English

Little Brown Jug

J. Winner
(1837–1918)

Hand in Hand

Mozart
(1756–91)

AB 3384V

Greek Wedding

Greek

Casey Jones

North American

The Boat to Inverie